GOODRICH MOVIE REVIEW

A Journey Through Emotional Healing and Family Bonds

MARCUS T. HOOKS

COPYRIGHT

Copyright©2024 Marcus T. Hooks. All rights reserved. No part of this publication may be reproduced, distributed, or transmitted in any form or by any means, including photocopying, recording, or other electronic or mechanical methods, without the prior written permission of the publisher, except in the case of brief quotations embodied in critical reviews and certain other non-commercial uses permitted by copyright law

TABLE OF CONTENTS

COPYRIGHT 1

TABLE OF CONTENTS 2

INTRODUCTION 3

    Goodrich Movie Review 3

CHAPTER 1 5

    Introduction to *Goodrich*: A Family Drama Unfolded ... 5

CHAPTER 2 12

    Plot Dissection: Understanding the Storyline 12

CHAPTER 3 21

    Character Analysis: Emotional Depths of Fatherhood .. 21

CHAPTER 4 31

    Themes and Symbolism in *Goodrich* 31

CHAPTER 5 43

    The Cinematic Experience: Direction, Cinematography, and Music 43

CHAPTER 6 55

    Cultural and Social Impact of *Goodrich* 55

CHAPTER 7 68

    The Role of Humor in *Goodrich* 68

CONCLUSION 77

    A Deep Dive into *Goodrich* – Family, Redemption, and Emotional Growth 77

INTRODUCTION
Goodrich Movie Review

Welcome to *Goodrich Movie Review*, an insightful exploration into Hallie Meyers-Shyer's 2024 family dramedy, *Goodrich*. This book aims to provide a comprehensive, in-depth analysis of the film, touching on its central themes, narrative structure, character development, and the broader social and cultural implications that make *Goodrich* a standout in contemporary cinema.

Goodrich presents a deeply relatable story of family dynamics, personal redemption, and the emotional struggles that accompany modern parenthood. Through its balance of humor and heartfelt drama, the film captivates audiences with its authenticity and emotional depth, making it a memorable cinematic experience. Starring Michael Keaton as Andy Goodrich, a man forced to confront his past failings as a father, the movie delves into the challenges of single parenthood, addiction recovery, and the possibility of second chances.

In this book, you'll find a detailed breakdown of the film's plot, characters, and themes, as well as an analysis of how humor is skillfully used to balance heavier moments. Each chapter is designed to offer a unique perspective on *Goodrich*, from its technical cinematic elements such as direction, cinematography, and music, to its relevance in addressing contemporary societal issues like blended families and mental health. Whether you are a casual moviegoer or a film enthusiast, this review will provide you with a deeper understanding of *Goodrich* and its lasting impact on both audiences and critics.

Join us on this journey through *Goodrich* as we dissect the film's powerful storytelling, its use of humor to engage audiences, and the meaningful lessons it imparts about family, forgiveness, and emotional growth.

CHAPTER 1

Introduction to *Goodrich*: A Family Drama Unfolded

The 2024 film Goodrich represents a poignant exploration of family, personal growth, and the complexities of modern life, wrapped in a comedic package. Written and directed by Hallie Meyers-Shyer, the film stars Michael Keaton in the lead role of Andy Goodrich, with a supporting cast including Mila Kunis, Andie MacDowell, and Carmen Ejogo. As a contemporary family drama, Goodrich navigates the turbulent waters of parenting, relationships, and self-discovery, combining humour with emotionally resonant themes that have the potential to speak to a broad audience.

Overview of the Film and Its Central Themes

Goodrich opens with the character of Andy Goodrich, a middle-aged Los Angeles art dealer whose life is upended when his much younger second wife enters a 90-day rehab program, leaving him to care for their twin nine-year-olds. Unprepared for the demands of single parenthood, Andy turns to his adult daughter, Grace (played by Mila Kunis), from a previous marriage, who is expecting her first child.

The film follows Andy as he navigates the often chaotic world of modern parenthood, while simultaneously attempting to mend his relationship with Grace, who harbours resentment for his absence during her upbringing.

The central themes of *Goodrich* revolve around family dynamics, personal growth, and the ongoing challenges of modern parenting. The film delves into the intricacies of fatherhood, exploring the evolution of Andy's relationship with his children as he moves from being emotionally distant to a more engaged and loving father. This growth is not only limited to his interactions with his twins, but also extends to his older daughter, as Andy strives to reconnect with her in a meaningful way.

The theme of second chances plays a crucial role in the narrative, as Andy is given the opportunity to redeem himself in the eyes of his children, particularly Grace. His character arc reflects a journey of self-discovery and redemption, as he confronts the mistakes of his past and works towards becoming the father he never was. At its core, *Goodrich* is a story about forgiveness, not only of others but also of oneself, and the idea that it is never too late to change.

The film also addresses the complexities of modern parenthood, particularly the challenges faced by single parents and those who are thrust into primary caregiving roles. Andy's struggle to balance his career with his newfound responsibilities as a single parent provides much of the film's comedic moments, as he fumbles through school drop-offs, parent-teacher meetings, and bedtime routines with little prior experience. However, these moments of humour are underscored by the deeper emotional struggles Andy faces as he learns to navigate the demands of parenting while grappling with his own insecurities.

Director's Vision and Inspiration Behind *Goodrich*

Hallie Meyers-Shyer, the writer and director of *Goodrich*, is no stranger to family-driven narratives. The daughter of filmmakers Nancy Meyers and Charles Shyer, she grew up surrounded by stories that centred on relationships, family, and personal growth. Her previous directorial debut, *Home Again* (2017), also focused on themes of family and self-discovery, though *Goodrich* takes a more mature and nuanced approach to these subjects.

In interviews, Meyers-Shyer has expressed that the inspiration behind *Goodrich* came from her observations of the shifting dynamics of family life in contemporary society. She noted how the traditional family structure has evolved, with more blended families and single-parent households becoming the norm. Meyers-Shyer wanted to explore how these changes impact not only parents but also children, and how individuals must learn to adapt to these new realities.

One of the key elements Meyers Shyer sought to highlight in *Goodrich* is the idea of personal transformation, particularly in the context of fatherhood. In a world where fathers are often portrayed as either absent or emotionally distant, Meyers-Shyer wanted to create a character who embodies the struggle many modern fathers face as they attempt to balance their careers with their responsibilities at home. Andy Goodrich's journey from a hands-off parent to a fully engaged father is at the heart of the film, and Meyers-Shyer handles this evolution with both humour and emotional depth.

Additionally, Meyers-Shyer's decision to infuse the film with comedic elements was a deliberate choice to make the heavier themes more accessible to a wider audience. While the film deals with serious issues, such as addiction, family estrangement, and the pressure of parenthood, the use of humour helps to alleviate the weight of these subjects, making the story both engaging and relatable. The comedic moments in the film are not simply there for levity but are integrated into the narrative in a way that feels organic and true to the characters' experiences.

Initial Audience Reception and Critical Reviews

Goodrich premiered in Los Angeles on October 8, 2024, at the AMC Grove 14, with a wider theatrical release set for October 18, 2024. The initial reception from both audiences and critics has been generally positive, with many praising the film's blend of humour and heart. Michael Keaton's performance as Andy Goodrich has garnered particular attention, with critics noting his ability to balance comedic timing with the more emotional beats of the film. Keaton, who has had a long and varied career, brings a sense of gravitas to the role, while also displaying his well-known comedic chops.

Critics have also lauded the film for its exploration of modern parenting and family dynamics, with many highlighting how *Goodrich* presents a realistic portrayal of the challenges faced by single parents. The film's ability to tackle serious themes, such as addiction and family estrangement, while still maintaining a light-hearted tone, has been praised as one of its strengths. The performances of the supporting cast, including Mila Kunis as Grace and Andie MacDowell as Andy's ex-wife, have also been well-received, with Kunis being singled out for her portrayal of a woman struggling to reconcile her feelings towards her father while preparing for the arrival of her own child.

However, not all reviews have been glowing. Some critics have pointed out that the film's reliance on certain comedic tropes, particularly in the portrayal of Andy's ineptitude as a parent, can sometimes feel predictable. While the film's humour is generally well-executed, there are moments where it borders on cliché, particularly in scenes that involve Andy's bumbling attempts to navigate modern parenting. That said, these critiques have been relatively minor, with most reviewers acknowledging that the film's emotional core more than makes up for any perceived shortcomings in the comedic execution.

Audiences have responded positively to the film's message of forgiveness and personal growth, with many viewers finding Andy's journey to be both relatable and inspiring. The film's focus on the importance of family and the idea that it is never too late to change has resonated with audiences, particularly those who have experienced similar challenges in their own lives. The film's blend of comedy and drama has made it an enjoyable and thought-provoking experience for a wide range of viewers, from parents to adult children and everyone in between.

Goodrich offers a refreshing take on the family drama genre, with its blend of humour, heart, and emotional depth. Hallie Meyers-Shyer's vision for the film, combined with strong performances from the cast, particularly Michael Keaton, has resulted in a film that is both entertaining and deeply resonant. While the film may rely on certain comedic tropes, its exploration of family dynamics, personal growth, and modern parenting challenges makes it a worthwhile addition to the genre. As *Goodrich* continues to reach a wider audience, it is likely to leave a lasting impact on viewers, reminding them of the importance of family, forgiveness, and second chances.

CHAPTER 2

Plot Dissection: Understanding the Storyline

Goodrich is a 2024 family comedy-drama that combines heartfelt moments with humorous undertones to deliver a compelling narrative about personal growth, family dynamics, and second chances. Directed by Hallie Meyers-Shyer, the film features Michael Keaton in the titular role as Andy Goodrich, a middle-aged art dealer whose life is thrown into disarray when his younger second wife enters a 90-day rehab program, leaving him to care for their nine-year-old twins. Throughout the film, *Goodrich* unpacks the challenges of modern parenthood, the complexities of estranged family relationships, and the evolution of a man who is forced to confront his shortcomings as a father and individual.

This chapter delves deeply into the film's storyline, covering key plot points, character arcs, and thematic elements. While maintaining the integrity of the narrative, we will explore how *Goodrich* resonates with contemporary family dynamics, addressing key moments, plot twists, and the pacing of the film.

Detailed Breakdown of the Storyline

Goodrich begins by introducing its protagonist, Andy Goodrich, a successful but somewhat emotionally distant art dealer based in Los Angeles. Andy has led a relatively comfortable life, largely detached from the day-to-day responsibilities of parenting. His second marriage, to a much younger woman, has been a source of stability, though he has remained somewhat disconnected from the rigors of raising their twin children. The film wastes no time setting the stage for the central conflict: Andy's wife, struggling with personal issues, decides to enter a 90-day rehabilitation program, leaving Andy to manage the children on his own.

This situation marks the beginning of Andy's journey, as he is thrust into a role he is neither prepared for nor particularly interested in. As the film unfolds, Andy's initial attempts at parenting are both comedic and painful to watch. He fumbles through daily routines, struggles to understand his children's needs, and often appears completely out of his depth. The early scenes of the film depict Andy as a man who is more comfortable in the world of art and business than in the intimate, chaotic space of family life.

The arrival of Grace, Andy's adult daughter from his first marriage, introduces a new layer of tension to the story.

Grace, played by Mila Kunis, is pregnant and on the verge of starting her own family. However, her relationship with Andy is strained due to his emotional absence during her childhood. Grace steps in to help Andy with the twins, but her presence serves as a constant reminder of his past failures as a father. This relationship forms the emotional core of the movie, as Andy and Grace navigate the rocky terrain of their shared history while learning to support each other in the present.

One of the key moments in the film occurs when Andy, overwhelmed by the demands of single parenthood, reaches out to Grace for help. This act of vulnerability is significant, as it represents a turning point in Andy's character arc. Throughout the film, Andy's interactions with Grace are marked by a sense of guilt and regret, and this moment allows him to begin the process of healing their fractured relationship. Grace, for her part, is initially reluctant to help, but as the film progresses, she begins to see her father's efforts to change and becomes more open to reconciliation.

As Andy becomes more involved in the lives of his twins, the film explores the challenges of balancing personal and professional responsibilities. The art world, which had once been Andy's refuge, now feels distant and unimportant compared to the demands of parenthood. The movie illustrates this shift in Andy's priorities through a series of small but significant moments, such as when he misses an important meeting to attend his children's school event. These moments serve to highlight Andy's growing understanding of what it means to be a parent and the sacrifices it entails.

The film's pacing is steady, allowing viewers to fully engage with Andy's gradual transformation. Unlike many family dramas that rely on dramatic, fast-paced developments, *Goodrich* takes its time to explore the subtleties of Andy's character growth. This slow-burn approach works in the film's favor, as it allows the audience to connect with Andy on a deeper level and witness the small but meaningful changes in his behavior. The narrative structure is linear, with a clear progression from Andy's initial resistance to his eventual acceptance of his role as a father.

Key Moments and Plot Twists

One of the film's most poignant moments occurs midway through the story when Andy, after a particularly difficult day, sits down with Grace to discuss their past. In this emotionally charged scene, Grace confronts Andy about his absence during her childhood and the impact it had on her life. This confrontation is a pivotal moment for both characters, as it forces Andy to acknowledge his mistakes and take responsibility for the hurt he caused. Grace's vulnerability in this scene also reveals the depth of her pain, and the exchange between father and daughter is raw and authentic.

Another key plot twist occurs when Andy's wife unexpectedly returns from rehab earlier than planned. Her return disrupts the new dynamic that Andy and the children have established, creating tension and uncertainty about the future of their family. This twist adds complexity to the narrative, as it forces Andy to confront not only his relationship with his children but also the unresolved issues in his marriage. The film does not offer easy answers to these challenges, instead opting for a more realistic portrayal of the difficulties of family life.

As the film moves toward its conclusion, Andy's growth as a father is evident. He becomes more attuned to his children's needs, and his relationship with Grace continues to improve. However, the film avoids a tidy, Hollywood-style resolution, instead presenting a more nuanced ending that reflects the ongoing nature of personal growth and family healing. Andy is not a perfect father by the end of the film, but he has made significant strides in becoming a more present and engaged parent.

The Film's Pacing and Narrative Structure

The pacing of *Goodrich* is deliberate and measured, allowing the story to unfold naturally without rushing through important emotional beats. This approach is particularly effective in a film that deals with complex family dynamics and personal growth, as it gives the characters the space they need to evolve. The narrative is structured around Andy's journey from reluctant father to a more engaged and self-aware parent, with each scene contributing to this overarching arc.

The film's structure is linear, with the plot unfolding in a straightforward manner. However, within this structure, there are moments of reflection and introspection that add depth to the narrative. Flashbacks to Andy's past, particularly his relationship with Grace during her childhood, are used sparingly but effectively to provide context for the present-day tensions between father and daughter. These flashbacks are not overly dramatic but serve to illustrate the long-standing issues that Andy must confront in order to move forward.

One of the strengths of the film's pacing is its ability to balance comedic moments with more serious emotional beats. The humor in *Goodrich* is organic and rooted in the characters' experiences, rather than feeling forced or out of place. This balance is crucial in a film that deals with heavy themes such as addiction, estrangement, and the pressures of parenthood. The comedic elements provide relief without undermining the emotional weight of the story, making the film feel both grounded and accessible.

How the Story Resonates with Contemporary Family Dynamics

At its core, *Goodrich* is a film about the complexities of family life and the ways in which relationships evolve over time. The film's portrayal of contemporary family dynamics is both realistic and relatable, particularly in its depiction of blended families, single parenthood, and the challenges of maintaining connections across generations.

One of the key themes in the film is the idea that family relationships are constantly shifting and require ongoing effort to maintain. Andy's journey as a father reflects the reality that parenting is not a static role, but one that evolves as both parents and children grow. His initial detachment from his children, followed by his gradual involvement in their lives, mirrors the experiences of many modern parents who struggle to balance work, personal growth, and family responsibilities.

The film also touches on the theme of generational differences and the impact they have on family dynamics. Andy's relationship with Grace is emblematic of the tension that can arise between parents and adult children, particularly when unresolved issues from the past come to the surface. Grace's own journey toward motherhood adds another layer of complexity to their relationship, as she must reconcile her feelings toward her father while preparing to take on the role of a parent herself.

Goodrich also resonates with contemporary audiences through its portrayal of addiction and recovery. Andy's wife's decision to enter rehab is a catalyst for the events of the film, and her struggle with addiction is treated with sensitivity and nuance. The film does not shy away from the impact that addiction can have on families, but it also offers a message of hope and redemption. Andy's growth as a father is mirrored by his wife's journey toward recovery, and both characters are shown to be capable of change and healing.

Goodrich offers a rich and layered narrative that explores the complexities of family life, personal growth, and the challenges of modern parenting. Through its detailed character development, measured pacing, and thoughtful exploration of contemporary themes, the film resonates with audiences on multiple levels. Andy Goodrich's journey from a detached father to a more engaged parent serves as a reminder that personal growth is an ongoing process, and that family relationships, while often difficult, are worth the effort to maintain and nurture. The film's blend of humor and heart makes it a compelling and relatable story for viewers of all ages, and its realistic portrayal of family dynamics ensures that it will leave a lasting impact on those who watch it.

CHAPTER 3

Character Analysis: Emotional Depths of Fatherhood

Goodrich is a film that hinges on the emotional growth and development of its characters, particularly its protagonist, Andy Goodrich. As a family comedy-drama, the movie explores complex relationships between parents and children, touching on themes of reconciliation, personal growth, and the messy dynamics of blended families. In this chapter, we'll dive deep into the character of Andy Goodrich, explore the supporting characters who shape the narrative, and discuss how each character grows and transforms throughout the film. Additionally, we'll analyse how the actors behind these roles brought depth and life to the story.

In-depth Exploration of Andy Goodrich, the Protagonist

Andy Goodrich, played by Michael Keaton, is the heart of the film. He begins the movie as a man whose life is seemingly under control. As an art dealer in Los Angeles, Andy has built a successful career, yet his personal life is far from perfect. He is emotionally distant from his two children from his second marriage, and he has a strained relationship with his adult daughter, Grace, from his first marriage. Andy's emotional detachment is a result of years of prioritising his work over his family, and this has left him ill-equipped to handle the responsibilities of fatherhood.

When Andy's younger wife enters a 90-day rehab program, Andy is suddenly thrust into the role of full-time caregiver for his nine-year-old twins. This marks the beginning of his journey toward self-awareness and personal growth. Throughout the film, Andy struggles with the demands of parenting, from mundane tasks like preparing meals and getting the children to school on time, to more significant emotional challenges, such as connecting with his children on a deeper level. His initial reluctance to take on these responsibilities is tempered by a growing realisation that he must change in order to become the father his children need.

What makes Andy's character so compelling is his gradual transformation. At the start of the film, he is disconnected, self-absorbed, and unwilling to confront the emotional needs of his family. However, as the story progresses, Andy begins to reflect on his past mistakes, particularly in his relationship with Grace. The film's emotional core is found in Andy's efforts to reconcile with his daughter, who feels abandoned by him during her childhood. Andy's arc is not one of instant redemption; instead, it is a slow and often painful process of self-examination and growth.

Michael Keaton's portrayal of Andy is both subtle and powerful. Known for his ability to balance humour with emotional depth, Keaton brings a layered performance that captures the complexities of fatherhood. He portrays Andy as a man who is both flawed and redeemable, and his journey toward becoming a better father feels authentic. Keaton's ability to convey vulnerability without losing the comedic undertones of the film is one of the key reasons why *Goodrich* succeeds in delivering a balanced narrative.

Supporting Characters and Their Contribution to the Narrative

While Andy Goodrich is the central figure, the supporting characters play a crucial role in shaping his journey. Each character represents a different aspect of Andy's life, and their interactions with him help to drive the narrative forward.

1. **Grace Goodrich (Mila Kunis)**: Grace is Andy's adult daughter from his first marriage, and her relationship with her father is one of the most emotionally charged aspects of the film. Grace is

pregnant and about to start her own family, yet she still carries the emotional scars of growing up with an absent father. Throughout the movie, Grace serves as a mirror for Andy's past mistakes, reminding him of the ways in which he failed her as a parent. However, Grace is not merely a victim; she is a strong, independent woman who is trying to reconcile her feelings toward her father while preparing to become a mother herself. Mila Kunis brings both strength and vulnerability to the role, and her performance is key to the emotional weight of the film.

2. **Andy's Twins**: Andy's nine-year-old twins from his second marriage are the catalyst for much of his personal growth. Initially, Andy views parenting as an obligation rather than a meaningful experience. However, as he spends more time with the twins, he begins to form genuine connections with them. The twins are portrayed as energetic and often mischievous, providing much of the film's comedic relief. Despite their antics, they represent the innocence and unconditional love that forces Andy to reevaluate his priorities.

3. **Andy's Wife**: Though she is absent for much of the film, Andy's younger wife, who is in rehab, serves as a critical plot point. Her decision to enter treatment forces Andy to take responsibility for the twins, setting the stage for his transformation. Her character is not fully fleshed out in the film, but her absence serves as a reminder of the challenges families face when dealing with issues such as addiction. The film does not portray her as a villain, but rather as a person struggling with her own demons, much like Andy is struggling with his shortcomings as a father.

4. **Supporting Cast (Andie MacDowell, Carmen Ejogo)**: Andie MacDowell and Carmen Ejogo play smaller but significant roles in the film. MacDowell portrays Andy's ex-wife and Grace's mother, adding another layer to the family dynamic. Her interactions with Andy are filled with the tension of past grievances, but there is also a sense of mutual understanding that develops over the course of the film. Ejogo plays a close family friend who offers Andy guidance and support as he navigates his new responsibilities. Both characters provide Andy with

perspectives that challenge him to become a better father and person.

Growth and Transformation of Characters Through the Movie

The growth and transformation of the characters in *Goodrich* is at the heart of the film's narrative. While Andy's journey is the most prominent, the supporting characters also experience their own moments of personal development.

- **Andy's Growth**: Andy's transformation is the most significant arc in the film. He begins as a man who is disconnected from his children and largely unaware of the emotional impact his absence has had on Grace. By the end of the film, Andy has become a more engaged and self-aware father. His journey is marked by small but meaningful moments, such as learning how to care for his twins' daily needs, attending their school events, and—most importantly—taking responsibility for the emotional well-being of his children. Andy's growth is not without setbacks, but his willingness to confront his past mistakes and make amends with Grace demonstrates his capacity for change.

- **Grace's Transformation**: Grace's growth is more subtle, but equally important. At the start of the film, she is hesitant to reconnect with her father, harbouring resentment for his absence during her childhood. However, as she sees Andy making an effort to change, Grace begins to soften. Her journey is one of forgiveness—not just of her father, but of herself as she prepares to become a mother. Grace's character arc is about learning to let go of the past and embracing the possibility of a better future for her own child.

- **The Twins**: While the twins are not as fully developed as Andy or Grace, they serve as symbols of innocence and the unconditional love that drives Andy's transformation. Their growth is more about their relationship with their father than any personal development of their own. As Andy becomes more involved in their lives, the twins begin to see him not as a distant figure, but as a parent who is present and caring. Their bond with Andy grows stronger as the film progresses, culminating in a final scene that suggests a hopeful future for the family.

How the Actors Brought These Roles to Life

The performances in *Goodrich* are one of the film's strongest aspects, with each actor bringing emotional depth and nuance to their roles.

- **Michael Keaton as Andy Goodrich**: Michael Keaton's portrayal of Andy is a masterclass in subtlety. Known for his ability to blend comedy with drama, Keaton infuses Andy with a sense of vulnerability that makes his journey toward redemption feel authentic. His comedic timing is impeccable, particularly in scenes where Andy is clearly out of his depth as a parent. However, it is Keaton's ability to convey the emotional weight of Andy's transformation that truly stands out. His performance is grounded in realism, and he never overplays the character's emotional moments, allowing the audience to connect with Andy on a deeper level.

- **Mila Kunis as Grace Goodrich**: Kunis delivers a powerful performance as Grace, a woman who is both strong and emotionally scarred. Her portrayal of Grace is layered, capturing the character's internal conflict as she grapples with her feelings toward her father. Kunis has a natural ability to convey both strength and vulnerability, and this duality is key to Grace's character arc. Her scenes with Keaton are some of the most emotionally charged in the film, and their chemistry is palpable.

- **Supporting Cast**: The supporting cast, including Andie MacDowell and Carmen Ejogo, provide strong performances that help to flesh out the film's world. MacDowell brings a sense of wisdom and maturity to her role as Andy's ex-wife, while Ejogo's character offers a more grounded perspective on the challenges of parenting. Both actresses add depth to the narrative, and their performances complement the emotional journey of the main characters.

In *Goodrich*, the characters are the driving force behind the film's narrative. Andy Goodrich's journey from a disconnected father to a more engaged and self-aware parent is at the heart of the story, and Michael Keaton's performance brings depth and authenticity to this transformation. The supporting characters, particularly Grace, play crucial roles in shaping Andy's growth, and their own journeys add emotional weight to the film. The actors behind these roles deliver nuanced performances that elevate the film beyond a final scene, showing a family that, while imperfect, is on a path to healing and reconciliation.

Overall, *Goodrich* is a film about growth, change, and the complicated, often messy dynamics of modern family life. Andy's journey from emotional detachment to meaningful connection with his children and Grace forms the core of the narrative. Michael Keaton's performance, along with the strong supporting cast, elevates the film, allowing it to explore these themes with both humor and heart.

CHAPTER 4
Themes and Symbolism in *Goodrich*

Goodrich is a richly layered film that explores several significant themes, such as family, mental health, redemption, and reconciliation. Directed by Hallie Meyers-Shyer, the movie blends comedy and drama to explore how the complexities of modern relationships affect individuals and families. Beneath the surface, the film employs subtle symbolism in its visuals and dialogue, enhancing the narrative's emotional depth. This chapter delves into these themes, as well as the nuanced storytelling elements that add layers to the viewing experience. At its core, *Goodrich* serves as a meditation on human flaws, personal growth, and the power of forgiveness.

The Film's Exploration of Family, Mental Health, and Redemption

Goodrich is, above all, a film about family and the evolving dynamics that come with changing circumstances. The family unit depicted in the movie is far from traditional: it is a blended family that has been fractured by divorce, emotional distance, and unspoken resentment. As the protagonist Andy Goodrich (played by Michael Keaton) tries to navigate his new role as the sole caregiver for his nine-year-old twins, the film examines the complexities of family life, particularly the relationships between parents and children.

The theme of **family** is explored from multiple angles. At the heart of the story is Andy's strained relationship with his adult daughter, Grace, from his first marriage. Grace, played by Mila Kunis, harbours deep-seated feelings of abandonment stemming from Andy's absence during her formative years. The film does not shy away from the difficult emotions that come with estrangement, and much of the story revolves around Andy's attempts to rebuild the relationship with Grace while simultaneously taking on new responsibilities as a father to his young children.

The film's depiction of **blended families** is particularly poignant in today's society, where many families are formed through second marriages or face the challenges of co-parenting. The tension between Andy's roles as a father to his younger children and his older daughter speaks to the broader challenges of balancing relationships in complex family structures. *Goodrich* addresses these challenges with both humour and empathy, making the family dynamics relatable and deeply human.

Alongside family, the film explores the theme of **mental health**, particularly through the subplot involving Andy's wife, who is in rehab for substance abuse. While the movie focuses primarily on Andy's journey, the presence of addiction and its impact on the family is a recurring undercurrent. The decision to send Andy's wife to rehab is not treated as a dramatic plot twist, but rather as a fact of life that must be dealt with—much like Andy's newfound parenting responsibilities. Through this subplot, *Goodrich* touches on the stigma surrounding addiction and the difficult road to recovery, both for individuals and their loved ones.

The theme of **redemption** is central to Andy's character arc. As a man who has made significant mistakes in the past—most notably in his relationship with Grace—Andy is given a second chance to become a better father. The film does not offer an idealised or simplified path to redemption; instead, it shows the messy, uncomfortable process of taking responsibility for past wrongs and working towards healing. Andy's journey is filled with setbacks and moments of self-doubt, but the film ultimately suggests that redemption is possible through effort, self-reflection, and genuine attempts to make amends.

Symbolism in Visuals and Dialogue

While *Goodrich* may appear to be a straightforward family drama on the surface, it is filled with subtle symbolism that adds depth to the narrative. The film uses both visual cues and dialogue to enhance its themes of growth, forgiveness, and the cyclical nature of family life.

One recurring symbol in the film is **art**, which serves as a metaphor for both creation and healing. As an art dealer, Andy's professional life revolves around the appreciation of artistic beauty, yet his personal life has been neglected. Throughout the film, there are several moments where Andy's profession is contrasted with his parenting responsibilities, highlighting the disconnect between his carefully curated public persona and the messy, unpredictable world of family life. This contrast is perhaps most evident in scenes where Andy is forced to choose between attending an art exhibition and caring for his children. The act of balancing these two worlds reflects

Andy's internal struggle to reconcile his career ambitions with his desire to be a better father.

Additionally, **art** serves as a visual representation of the healing process. There is a scene in which Andy helps his children create a piece of artwork, symbolising the idea that relationships, like art, require time, effort, and creativity to rebuild. This moment of bonding is a turning point for Andy, as it signifies his growing commitment to his children and his willingness to invest in their emotional well-being.

Another key symbol in the film is the **rehabilitation center**, where Andy's wife is staying. Although she is physically absent for much of the film, the rehab center serves as a constant reminder of the need for self-care and the work required to address personal flaws. Just as Andy's wife is undergoing a process of healing, so too is Andy in his own way. The film subtly draws parallels between the recovery process and the emotional work Andy must do to rebuild his relationships with his children and Grace. The rehab center represents both a place of recovery and a place of distance—Andy is forced to confront his role in his wife's absence and reflect on how their strained relationship affects the family.

Dialogue also plays a significant role in conveying the film's deeper meanings. Throughout *Goodrich*, the characters engage in conversations that hint at larger themes without explicitly stating them. For example, when Grace confronts Andy about his past failures, their dialogue is filled with tension, but it also reveals the emotional scars that have yet to heal. The use of silence in these moments—pauses between sentences, the reluctance to say certain words—speaks volumes about the unspoken resentments that exist within families. The film allows its characters to express themselves through their actions and body language, often saying more in what they do not say than in what they verbalise.

Subtle Nuances That Add Depth to the Viewing Experience

Goodrich is a film that rewards careful viewers with its attention to subtle details and nuances. From the set design to the character interactions, the film is filled with small touches that add depth to the story and enrich the viewing experience.

One such nuance is the **use of space** in the film. The physical settings—Andy's art gallery, the family home, and the rehab center—are all designed to reflect the emotional states of the characters. Andy's art gallery, with its clean lines and carefully curated pieces, represents his desire for control and order, in contrast to the chaos of his home life. The family home, in particular, is often depicted as cluttered and disorganised, symbolising the disarray in Andy's personal life. As the film progresses and Andy becomes more involved in his children's lives, the home becomes a more welcoming and warm space, reflecting the gradual healing of the family unit.

Another subtle detail that adds depth to the film is the **use of time**. The film's pacing is deliberate, allowing the audience to feel the passage of time as Andy slowly becomes more attuned to his children's needs. This sense of time is mirrored in the narrative structure, as Andy's growth unfolds in small, incremental steps. The film does not rush to resolve the family's issues, instead opting for a more realistic portrayal of how relationships evolve over time. This slow-burn approach allows the audience to fully engage with the characters' emotional journeys, making the moments of reconciliation all the more powerful.

The film also employs **symbolic actions** that may seem inconsequential at first but carry significant emotional weight. For instance, a scene in which Andy struggles to prepare breakfast for his children is not just played for laughs—it is a reflection of his initial inability to take on the role of caregiver. Later in the film, when Andy successfully makes a meal for his children, the action takes on a deeper meaning, symbolising his growth as a father and his newfound competence in the role.

The Underlying Message About Reconciliation and Human Flaws

At its core, *Goodrich* is a film about reconciliation—both with others and with oneself. The movie's central message is that human beings are inherently flawed, but through effort, reflection, and forgiveness, they can find a path to healing.

The theme of **reconciliation** is most evident in Andy's relationship with Grace. Throughout the film, Grace's anger toward her father is palpable, and for much of the story, it seems as though their relationship may never be repaired. However, the film suggests that reconciliation is possible, even in the most fractured relationships, as long as both parties are willing to make the effort. Andy's willingness to admit his mistakes and actively work toward rebuilding his relationship with Grace is a testament to the film's belief in the power of forgiveness.

Goodrich also explores the idea of **self-reconciliation**. Andy's journey is not just about making amends with his family, but also about coming to terms with his own flaws and learning to forgive himself. The film acknowledges that personal growth is difficult and often uncomfortable, but it is also necessary for healing. Andy's character arc is a reminder that self-awareness and self-compassion are crucial components of any redemption story.

Ultimately, the film's underlying message is one of **hope**. While the characters in *Goodrich* are far from perfect, the movie suggests that people are capable of change and that even the most broken relationships can be mended with time and effort. The film does not offer easy answers or quick fixes, but it does provide a sense of optimism about the possibility of reconciliation. In a world where family dynamics are often fraught with tension and misunderstandings, *Goodrich* offers a hopeful vision of how individuals can overcome their flaws and find redemption in the process. *Goodrich* offers a hopeful vision of how individuals can overcome their flaws and find redemption in the context of family relationships.

The idea that people can evolve, despite their mistakes, is illustrated through the relationships between Andy and his children, and between Andy and himself. At the beginning of the film, Andy is a flawed character—absent, distracted, and emotionally unavailable—but he grows into someone who acknowledges his limitations and works to be better. This growth is gradual and comes with setbacks, but it is depicted in a way that feels authentic and grounded in reality.

The film makes it clear that reconciliation requires **effort and vulnerability**. Andy's relationship with Grace is especially challenging because of the emotional scars from the past. Grace, hurt by her father's neglect, is initially hesitant to allow him back into her life. But as Andy shows a willingness to change, Grace begins to soften, and their relationship becomes a central focus of the film's message about forgiveness. The underlying message is that reconciliation is a process—it doesn't happen overnight and isn't always smooth. However, with patience and genuine effort, even deeply fractured relationships can heal.

In the context of **human flaws**, *Goodrich* acknowledges that no one is perfect. The film doesn't shy away from showing Andy's imperfections—his initial reluctance to embrace his parenting duties, his awkward attempts at bonding with his children, and his emotional distance from Grace. These flaws make Andy a relatable character and highlight the film's broader message about personal growth. Instead of portraying Andy as a one-dimensional character who suddenly becomes the perfect father, the film shows his struggles and gradual progress, emphasising that growth is an ongoing journey.

Moreover, the film also portrays other characters as complex individuals with their own imperfections. Grace's initial anger and reluctance to forgive her father demonstrate that she, too, is grappling with her emotions and trying to navigate the complicated relationship dynamics. The twins, though innocent, represent the challenges of raising children and how parenting is a constant learning process. Even Andy's wife, whose presence is more felt than seen, is a representation of the flaws that exist in every family. Her decision to seek help for her addiction is a powerful subplot that reinforces the idea that healing and redemption are possible, but they require acknowledgment of one's flaws.

The film's subtle approach to conveying these themes resonates deeply with audiences because it reflects the complexities of real life. Families are messy, relationships are imperfect, and people are flawed—but through honesty, self-reflection, and perseverance, reconciliation and redemption can be achieved. *Goodrich* doesn't present a picture-perfect resolution, but it does offer hope that people can change for the better and that relationships, no matter how damaged, can be repaired over time.

In conclusion, *Goodrich* masterfully weaves together the themes of family, mental health, redemption, and reconciliation. Through its nuanced portrayal of human flaws, the film offers a hopeful message about the power of forgiveness and the possibility of healing even the most broken relationships. The symbolism in visuals and dialogue enhances the emotional depth of the narrative, while the subtle details and nuanced performances by the cast add richness to the viewing experience. Ultimately, *Goodrich* reminds us that personal growth is a lifelong journey, and that reconciliation—whether with family, friends, or oneself—is always possible, as long as there is a willingness to face the past and embrace change.

CHAPTER 5
The Cinematic Experience: Direction, Cinematography, and Music

In *Goodrich*, the story's emotional depth is amplified by the technical elements of the filmmaking process, including direction, cinematography, and music. These elements play a crucial role in shaping how the narrative unfolds and how the audience connects with the characters and themes. Under the direction of Hallie Meyers-Shyer, *Goodrich* combines visually engaging cinematography with a carefully curated soundtrack that enhances the emotional beats of the film. This chapter examines the filmmaking techniques used in *Goodrich*, with an emphasis on direction, cinematography, music, and visual storytelling.

Direction Style and Choices by the Filmmaker

Hallie Meyers-Shyer's approach to *Goodrich* reflects her background in relationship-driven narratives, focusing on emotional honesty and subtle, relatable moments. As the daughter of filmmakers Nancy Meyers and Charles Shyer, Meyers-Shyer brings a particular sensitivity to the dynamics of family relationships, a hallmark of her directorial style.

Her work on *Goodrich* is not about creating grandiose, dramatic moments, but instead about finding the emotional truth in the ordinary events of life. This is most apparent in the way she handles the interactions between the characters, allowing their dialogue and actions to flow naturally, without over-directing or forcing emotional peaks.

Meyers-Shyer's direction in *Goodrich* is focused on **character-driven storytelling**. The film places its characters at the forefront, and her choices emphasise the gradual evolution of Andy Goodrich (Michael Keaton) as a father and individual. Meyers-Shyer allows the camera to linger on the characters during quiet moments, giving the audience time to connect with them on an emotional level. Rather than rushing through scenes, she uses pacing to let the characters breathe, making their transformation feel genuine and earned.

A notable element of Meyers-Shyer's direction is her use of **comedy** to offset the film's more serious themes. In keeping with the genre of family dramedy, *Goodrich* balances moments of levity with more emotionally charged scenes. Meyers-Shyer achieves this balance by allowing humour to arise naturally from the characters' interactions, rather than relying on forced comedic setups. For example, Andy's fumbling attempts at parenthood provide comedic relief, but they also serve to deepen the audience's understanding of his journey. These moments of lightness never detract from the emotional weight of the story; instead, they enhance the relatability of the characters and the situations they find themselves in.

Additionally, Meyers-Shyer's decision to focus on **subtle character growth** rather than grand emotional arcs aligns with the film's theme of incremental change. The direction allows the audience to witness Andy's development in small, meaningful ways. Whether it's his increasingly confident handling of his children's daily routines or his gradual reconnection with his estranged daughter, Grace (Mila Kunis), these moments of growth are depicted with restraint, avoiding melodrama and emphasising realism.

Cinematography and How It Enhances the Narrative

The cinematography in *Goodrich* is a key aspect of how the story is visually conveyed. Cinematographer Jamie D. Ramsay brings a naturalistic, warm visual aesthetic to the film, which complements the intimate and personal nature of the story. The film's visual style enhances the emotional undertones of the narrative by creating a sense of familiarity and comfort, inviting the audience into the world of the Goodrich family.

One of the defining features of the cinematography in *Goodrich* is the **use of space and framing** to reflect character dynamics. Throughout the film, the framing of scenes subtly conveys the emotional distance or closeness between characters. For instance, in early scenes where Andy struggles to connect with his children, the cinematography often frames him separately from them, highlighting the physical and emotional distance between them. Wide shots are used to emphasise the gaps in their relationships, with Andy frequently positioned at the edge of the frame while his children occupy the center. As the film progresses and Andy becomes more involved in his children's lives, the framing shifts to place him closer to them, symbolising his emotional growth and increasing presence in their world.

The **use of lighting** in *Goodrich* also plays a significant role in reinforcing the film's themes. The lighting is predominantly soft and warm, creating a visually inviting atmosphere that mirrors the film's exploration of family warmth and reconciliation. There is a notable contrast between the cool, sterile lighting of Andy's art gallery and the warmer tones used in the family home. This contrast visually represents Andy's transition from a detached, work-focused individual to a more emotionally engaged father. The family home, depicted with golden hues and softer shadows, becomes a space where healing and connection take place, while the art gallery serves as a symbol of Andy's previous life, where emotional distance prevailed.

Close-ups are frequently used in the film to capture the emotional subtleties of the characters' interactions. Meyers-Shyer and Ramsay utilise these intimate shots to draw the audience into the characters' emotional states, particularly during pivotal moments of vulnerability. For instance, when Andy has heartfelt conversations with Grace, the camera lingers on their faces, allowing the audience to witness the raw emotions of guilt, regret, and eventual forgiveness. These close-ups provide insight into the characters' internal struggles without the need for excessive dialogue, relying on facial expressions and body language to convey meaning.

The cinematography also contributes to the film's pacing, which is deliberately measured to reflect the slow, steady process of personal growth and family healing. The camera moves with a natural flow, avoiding rapid cuts or overly dramatic shifts. This allows the audience to remain immersed in the story, experiencing the characters' journey in real time rather than through heightened cinematic techniques. The decision to use **naturalistic lighting** and **steady camerawork** reinforces the film's grounded approach to its themes, making the characters' development feel more authentic and relatable.

The Impact of Music and Sound in Building Emotional Tension

The musical score for *Goodrich* was composed by Christopher Willis, whose previous work includes scores for both animated and live-action films. In *Goodrich*, Willis's score complements the film's tonal shifts between comedy and drama, enhancing the emotional weight of key moments without overwhelming the audience.

One of the primary ways music is used in *Goodrich* is to **underscore the emotional journey of the protagonist**. Andy's evolution from a detached father to a more engaged parent is mirrored in the score's progression, with light, playful melodies accompanying his early, comedic struggles with parenthood. These early scenes are scored with a whimsical touch, reflecting Andy's initial ineptitude and the humour that arises from his fumbling attempts to take care of his children. However, as the film delves deeper into the more serious themes of reconciliation and personal growth, the score shifts to more reflective, poignant tones.

The **use of music to build emotional tension** is particularly effective in scenes where Andy confronts his past mistakes. For example, during moments of introspection or when Andy and Grace engage in difficult conversations about their fractured relationship, the music takes on a more sombre and melancholic quality. The delicate piano notes and strings create an atmosphere of vulnerability, encouraging the audience to empathise with the characters' emotional pain. Willis's score never overshadows the dialogue but instead enhances the emotional resonance of these key scenes, helping to draw the audience into the characters' internal worlds.

Music also plays a role in **creating thematic continuity** throughout the film. Certain musical motifs recur during pivotal moments, reinforcing the film's central themes of family and redemption. For instance, a soft, recurring melody is associated with moments of bonding between Andy and his children, subtly reminding the audience of the emotional thread that runs through the film. This musical motif evolves as Andy's relationship with his children deepens, becoming more complex and layered as the film progresses.

In addition to the score, the film makes effective use of **diegetic sound** to enhance the realism of the family's daily life. The sounds of the home children's laughter, the clattering of dishes, and the hum of everyday activity—create an immersive auditory environment that grounds the story in the realities of parenthood. These sounds serve as a backdrop to Andy's journey, reinforcing the notion that his personal growth is happening within the context of real, everyday family life.

The use of **silence** is another important sound element in *Goodrich*. During moments of emotional tension, such as the confrontations between Andy and Grace, the absence of music creates a stark, quiet atmosphere that heightens the intensity of their conversations. By stripping away background noise and music during these scenes, Meyers-Shyer and Willis allow the weight of the characters' words to take center stage, amplifying the emotional impact.

Visual Storytelling Techniques Used in *Goodrich*

Goodrich employs a variety of visual storytelling techniques that enhance the narrative without relying heavily on exposition or dialogue. These techniques allow the film to convey meaning through imagery, providing a richer viewing experience for the audience.

One of the most prominent visual storytelling techniques in the film is the **use of mirrors and reflections**. Throughout the film, Andy is often shown looking at himself in mirrors or through reflective surfaces. These moments serve as a metaphor for his introspection and self-examination. As Andy grapples with his past mistakes and his evolving role as a father, these visual reflections highlight his internal struggle to reconcile his old self with the person he is becoming. The mirrors represent both literal and figurative self-reflection, underscoring the theme of personal growth.

The film also makes use of **symbolic objects** to convey deeper meaning. For example, one recurring symbol in the film is a set of framed family photographs that hang in Andy's home. These photographs, which depict moments of happiness from his past, serve as a visual reminder of the family relationships that have deteriorated over time…have deteriorated over time. These objects are strategically placed in scenes where Andy is confronted with his past failures, serving as a silent commentary on the state of his family relationships. As the film progresses, the positioning of these photos subtly shifts, mirroring Andy's emotional journey. By the end of the film, the photographs, once symbols of a fractured family, take on a new significance as Andy begins to rebuild his relationships with his children and Grace.

Another important visual motif in *Goodrich* is **the use of open and closed doors**. Throughout the film, doors are used to symbolise the barriers between Andy and his family. Early in the movie, closed doors often separate Andy from his children, representing his emotional distance from them. As Andy becomes more involved in their lives, doors are increasingly shown open, symbolising the breaking down of emotional barriers and the opening of new possibilities for connection and understanding. In particular, the scene where Grace finally opens the door to Andy's emotional overtures is a powerful moment of reconciliation, with the visual metaphor underscoring the progress they have made in their relationship.

Meyers-Shyer also uses **color symbolism** to underscore the film's themes of personal growth and family connection. For instance, the color palette of Andy's art gallery is dominated by cool, muted tones—grays, whites, and blues—reflecting the detached and sterile environment that he has created for himself. In contrast, the scenes set in the family home are filled with warm colors—yellows, oranges, and soft greens—representing the emotional warmth that is gradually returning to Andy's life as he reconnects with his family. This contrast between cool and warm tones visually represents Andy's internal journey from emotional detachment to emotional engagement.

Another key visual storytelling technique in *Goodrich* is **the framing of characters within their environments**. At various points in the film, Andy is shown framed by doorways, windows, or other architectural elements, isolating him visually from the rest of the family. This framing technique visually conveys Andy's isolation and emotional distance from his children and Grace. As the film progresses, the framing shifts, with Andy increasingly shown in more open, integrated spaces, symbolising his growing connection to his family. The shift in framing reflects the film's overall theme of emotional openness and the healing of family relationships.

Goodrich is a film that excels in its use of direction, cinematography, and music to enhance its narrative and emotional impact. Hallie Meyers-Shyer's direction focuses on character-driven storytelling, allowing the performances and interactions to unfold naturally, while the cinematography by Jamie D. Ramsay uses visual motifs and symbolic framing to deepen the film's exploration of family dynamics and personal growth. Christopher Willis's score complements the film's tonal shifts, providing both light-hearted and poignant moments that enhance the emotional depth of the story. Together, these elements create a rich cinematic experience that resonates with audiences, offering both humor and heartfelt exploration of themes such as redemption, forgiveness, and the complexities of family life. The visual storytelling techniques used in *Goodrich* add layers of meaning to the film, making it a compelling and emotionally rewarding experience for viewers.

CHAPTER 6
Cultural and Social Impact of *Goodrich*

Goodrich is more than just a family dramedy—it's a reflection of many of the struggles and cultural shifts that modern society grapples with today. The film's exploration of family, redemption, mental health, and the challenges of balancing personal and professional responsibilities positions it as a significant piece of commentary on the complexities of contemporary life. In this chapter, we will examine the cultural and social relevance of *Goodrich*, how it addresses modern family dynamics, the public and critical reactions to its portrayal of sensitive themes, and its lasting impact on audiences.

The Film's Relevance to Modern Societal Issues

At its core, *Goodrich* addresses several key societal issues that are particularly relevant in today's world. These include the challenges of single parenthood, the impact of addiction on families, and the evolving nature of family structures. The film's central theme of personal redemption and the possibility of second chances also resonates deeply in a society that increasingly values personal growth and emotional resilience.

1. The Changing Face of Parenthood

One of the most significant cultural conversations explored in *Goodrich* is the evolving role of parenthood, especially fatherhood. In recent years, there has been a growing recognition of the importance of fathers being emotionally present and engaged in their children's lives, rather than adhering to traditional gender roles that often position fathers as breadwinners rather than caregivers. *Goodrich* taps into this evolving conversation by depicting Andy, a father who is largely disconnected from his children at the start of the film, as he learns to take on a more active role in their upbringing.

Andy's initial struggles to adapt to the responsibilities of single parenthood reflect the experiences of many parents, particularly fathers, who find themselves navigating these challenges for the first time. The film speaks to the broader societal shift toward **shared parenting responsibilities**, emphasising that parenting is not just a mother's domain but requires the active participation of fathers as well. This message aligns with modern values around gender equality and family participation, offering a critique of outdated stereotypes while promoting a more inclusive vision of family life.

2. The Impact of Addiction and Mental Health

Another significant theme in *Goodrich* is the exploration of **addiction and mental health**. Andy's wife's decision to enter rehab early in the film sets the stage for the rest of the story, highlighting how addiction can disrupt the lives of entire families. The film's handling of this sensitive subject is both empathetic and realistic—it does not vilify Andy's wife but instead presents her decision to seek help as a necessary and courageous step toward healing.

The portrayal of addiction in *Goodrich* is timely, as discussions surrounding mental health and substance abuse have become increasingly prominent in recent years. The film sheds light on the ripple effects of addiction, showing how it forces family members to adjust their lives, confront their own emotional baggage, and ultimately find a way to rebuild their relationships. By presenting addiction and recovery as central to the story, *Goodrich* encourages conversations about mental health and the importance of supporting loved ones through difficult times.

3. Blended Families and Divorce

The structure of the family in *Goodrich*—a blended family that has been impacted by divorce—also speaks to modern societal trends. Divorce rates remain high, and many families today consist of step-parents, half-siblings, and other complex family configurations. The film acknowledges the challenges that come with these arrangements, particularly in the strained relationship between Andy and his adult daughter, Grace.

Grace's resentment toward her father for being absent during her childhood is a reflection of the emotional scars that can result from broken family structures. However, the film's ultimate message of reconciliation and the possibility of healing suggests that these wounds can be repaired over time. In this way, *Goodrich* offers a hopeful vision of how blended families can find their way toward unity, even after years of estrangement.

How *Goodrich* Engages with Contemporary Family Struggles

Goodrich is particularly adept at engaging with the **real-life struggles** that many families face, making it a relatable and emotionally resonant film for a wide audience. Through its depiction of Andy's journey, the film delves into the complexities of parenthood, divorce, and the difficulties of maintaining family bonds in a fast-paced, modern world.

1. Single Parenthood and Work-Life Balance

One of the central struggles that *Goodrich* addresses is the challenge of **single parenthood**, particularly for individuals who are thrust into this role unexpectedly. Andy's character arc—from a man who has largely avoided the responsibilities of parenting to someone who becomes fully engaged in his children's lives—mirrors the experiences of many single parents today. The film highlights the difficulties of balancing professional obligations with the demands of raising children, a challenge that is compounded when one parent is absent.

This struggle is particularly relevant in a society where many parents, both men and women, are juggling **careers and family responsibilities**. As the traditional model of the stay-at-home parent continues to shift, *Goodrich* reflects the reality of parents trying to find time for both work and family life, often feeling stretched thin in the process. The film's depiction of Andy's attempts to manage his art gallery while caring for his children speaks to the challenges faced by many modern parents who are expected to excel in both the professional and personal spheres.

2. Emotional Distance and Reconnection

Another key aspect of the film's engagement with contemporary family struggles is its exploration of **emotional distance** and the efforts to reconnect with estranged family members. Andy's strained relationship with Grace, his adult daughter from his first marriage, serves as a powerful example of how emotional neglect can have lasting effects on family bonds.

However, *Goodrich* also offers a hopeful message about the possibility of reconciliation, even after years of estrangement. Grace's initial reluctance to forgive her father gradually gives way to a more open and understanding relationship as she sees Andy making genuine efforts to change. This storyline resonates with many viewers who have experienced similar struggles in their own families—whether with estranged parents, siblings, or children. The film underscores the importance of forgiveness and the idea that it is never too late to repair broken relationships.

Public and Critic Reactions to the Film's Portrayal of Sensitive Themes

The public and critical reactions to *Goodrich* have been largely positive, particularly regarding its portrayal of sensitive themes such as family dynamics, addiction, and reconciliation. While the film has been praised for its warmth and emotional honesty, some critics have noted that its approach to these themes is more understated than one might expect, avoiding melodrama in favor of subtle character development and quiet moments of introspection.

1. Public Reception

Many viewers have connected deeply with the film's portrayal of family struggles, finding it to be a realistic and empathetic reflection of the challenges they face in their own lives. Audiences have praised *Goodrich* for its **relatable characters** and the authenticity of its emotional beats, particularly in how it handles the complexities of father-daughter relationships.

The depiction of **Andy's growth as a father** has resonated with both parents and adult children alike, with many viewers expressing appreciation for the film's message that it is never too late to make amends and become a better parent. The film's balanced tone, which blends humor with heartfelt moments, has also been a point of praise, making it accessible to a wide range of audiences.

2. Critical Reception

Critics have been similarly positive in their reviews of *Goodrich*, highlighting its nuanced handling of difficult subjects. Many have noted that the film's avoidance of heavy-handedness in its exploration of addiction and family conflict is one of its strengths. Rather than resorting to melodramatic plot twists, *Goodrich* allows its characters to evolve naturally, giving the film a sense of realism that sets it apart from more conventional family dramas.

Some critics have pointed out that the film's **deliberate pacing** and subtle approach to its themes may not appeal to all viewers, particularly those looking for a more dramatic or fast-paced narrative. However, for those who appreciate character-driven storytelling and emotional authenticity, *Goodrich* has been widely regarded as a thoughtful and impactful film.

3. Portrayal of Addiction and Recovery

One area where *Goodrich* has received particular acclaim is in its portrayal of **addiction and recovery**. Unlike many films that focus on the dramatic consequences of addiction, *Goodrich* takes a more restrained approach, focusing instead on the ripple effects that addiction can have on a family. By showing how Andy's wife's decision to enter rehab impacts him and their children, the film encourages viewers to think about the broader social and emotional implications of addiction, rather than just the individual struggle.

This portrayal has been praised by both critics and audiences for its empathy and nuance. Rather than depicting addiction as a moral failing or source of shame, the film presents it as a difficult but manageable challenge that requires support, understanding, and patience from loved ones. The film's message about the importance of seeking help and working toward recovery has resonated with viewers who have experienced similar situations in their own families, adding to its cultural relevance.

Lasting Impact on Viewers and Its Potential for Future Recognition

The lasting impact of *Goodrich* lies in its ability to speak to universal human experiences while grounding its story in the specific struggles of contemporary family life. The film's exploration of personal growth, forgiveness, and the complexities of family relationships has left a profound impression on many viewers, who see their own experiences reflected in the characters' journeys.

1. Emotional Resonance with Viewers

The emotional resonance of *Goodrich* has been one of its defining features, and it is likely to be a film that stays with viewers long after they leave the theater. Many audience members have noted how the film's exploration of **forgiveness and reconciliation** touched them on a personal level, prompting them to reflect on...how they handle relationships with their own parents, children, or partners. For many, the film's message of hope and redemption resonates deeply, particularly in its assertion that even the most fractured relationships can be healed with effort and understanding. The film's realistic portrayal of family dynamics, coupled with its focus on personal growth, has made it a source of comfort and reflection for audiences navigating their own familial challenges.

Goodrich has the potential for long-lasting cultural recognition due to its **timeless themes** of forgiveness, personal growth, and the importance of family. While the specific circumstances of the characters may be rooted in contemporary issues, such as addiction and single parenthood, the emotional core of the film is universal. The film's emphasis on reconciliation and second chances ensures that it will remain relevant as long as families continue to face the same struggles with communication, forgiveness, and healing.

2. Potential for Awards and Recognition

While *Goodrich* may not be the type of film that dominates blockbuster charts, its **emotional depth** and thoughtful execution have positioned it as a strong contender for future recognition in the world of independent cinema and family dramas. Michael Keaton's portrayal of Andy Goodrich has been widely praised, and there is potential for him to receive acting nominations in awards circuits for his nuanced, heartfelt performance. The film's ability to balance comedy with emotional gravity could also garner attention in categories such as screenwriting, direction, and even music composition for its carefully crafted score.

Additionally, *Goodrich* is likely to find a lasting place in discussions about **films that explore family dynamics**. Much like other character-driven dramas that focus on personal transformation, *Goodrich* may continue to be referenced in future conversations about films that authentically depict the messiness of real-life relationships, with all their flaws and opportunities for redemption.

Goodrich is a film that not only entertains but also reflects on significant cultural and social issues, making it a relevant and impactful contribution to the cinematic landscape. By addressing modern family dynamics, mental health, addiction, and personal growth, the film resonates with audiences navigating similar struggles in their own lives. Its portrayal of the complexities of fatherhood, reconciliation, and emotional healing offers a relatable and hopeful vision for families dealing with difficult situations. The film's subtle direction, naturalistic cinematography, and emotionally evocative score further enhance its impact, ensuring that *Goodrich* will have a lasting effect on its viewers and stand as a memorable, thought-provoking piece of cinema. Whether through public acclaim or future recognition in the form of awards and critical discourse,

Goodrich has made a meaningful mark on its audience and the cultural conversation around modern family life.

CHAPTER 7
The Role of Humor in *Goodrich*

The role of humor in *Goodrich* plays a significant part in balancing the film's dramatic elements with lighter, more relatable moments. Throughout the movie, humor serves multiple functions: it relieves tension during emotionally charged scenes, underscores character development, and engages the audience, making the film more accessible to a wider demographic. By blending comedy with heavier themes such as family conflict, redemption, and addiction, *Goodrich* avoids becoming overly solemn or weighed down by its serious subject matter. Instead, the humor brings levity to the narrative, ensuring that the audience remains invested in the characters and their journeys.

Balancing Comedy with Drama

One of the standout aspects of *Goodrich* is how deftly it balances humor with the more serious, emotionally driven moments of the film. This balance is critical in making the film relatable to audiences, who may otherwise find its focus on family dysfunction and personal failure overwhelming. The use of comedy allows the film to maintain an approachable tone while still addressing deeper emotional truths.

The comedy in *Goodrich* largely arises from situational humor, particularly Andy Goodrich's (played by Michael Keaton) initial ineptitude as a single father. Early in the movie, Andy is forced to take on the role of primary caregiver for his nine-year-old twins when his younger second wife enters rehab. Andy, who has previously lived a life removed from the day-to-day realities of parenting, is suddenly thrust into a world of school drop-offs, meal planning, and tantrums. His struggles with these new responsibilities are ripe for comedic moments, which the film capitalizes on to keep the tone light. For instance, Andy's first attempt at preparing breakfast for his children is a disaster, with burnt toast and spilled juice taking center stage. His clumsy efforts to manage the mundane tasks of parenting bring laughter to the audience, even as they highlight his emotional distance from his children.

This juxtaposition between humor and emotional distance is a hallmark of *Goodrich*. While Andy's initial failures as a parent are humorous, they also serve to underscore his detachment and lack of familiarity with his children's needs. The comedy in these scenes is not just about making the audience laugh—it's about revealing Andy's character and setting the stage for his eventual growth. As Andy slowly becomes more involved in his children's lives, the humor begins to shift as well. The film transitions from laughing at Andy's incompetence to finding humor in the ordinary, relatable moments of family life. This shift reflects the broader emotional journey of the film, as Andy's relationship with his children deepens and becomes more meaningful.

Another example of the balance between comedy and drama occurs in Andy's interactions with his adult daughter, Grace (played by Mila Kunis). Grace's resentment toward her father for being absent during her childhood is a serious source of tension in the film, but *Goodrich* does not dwell in this darkness for too long. Instead, the film uses moments of humor to relieve the tension and make their relationship feel more real and dynamic. In one scene, Grace sarcastically comments on her father's newfound parenting efforts, saying, "Who knew you'd become the next Dr. Spock?" while Andy awkwardly tries to navigate a conversation about raising kids. These moments of levity help to humanize the characters, preventing their interactions from becoming overly melodramatic or heavy-handed.

In this way, *Goodrich* effectively balances comedy with drama, using humor to complement rather than undercut the film's emotional depth. The humor is never forced or out of place; instead, it arises naturally from the characters' personalities and the situations they find themselves in. This careful integration of humor allows the film to explore difficult themes—such as addiction, estrangement, and the struggle for personal redemption—without overwhelming the audience.

Humor as a Reflection of Character Growth

In *Goodrich*, humor is not just a tool for entertainment; it also serves as a reflection of Andy's character growth over the course of the film. Early on, much of the humor is derived from Andy's bumbling attempts at parenthood. He is a man who is completely out of his element, and his awkwardness in this role generates much of the film's early comedy. However, as Andy begins to evolve and become more comfortable with his responsibilities, the humor shifts, reflecting his development as a character.

At the start of the film, Andy's comedic moments are largely situational, arising from his incompetence as a parent. He burns food, forgets to pick his children up from school, and generally stumbles through the basics of fatherhood. These early scenes depict Andy as a man who is disconnected from his children and unsure of how to fulfill his role as a father. The humor in these moments is often physical and broad, emphasizing Andy's discomfort and lack of preparedness.

As the film progresses, however, the humor becomes more relational, arising from the interactions between Andy and his children rather than from his failures. This shift in humor mirrors Andy's growth as a parent. He moves from being an awkward, detached figure to someone who is more emotionally present and capable of engaging with his children on their level. For example, in one scene later in the film, Andy plays a board game with his twins, and the humor comes from their playful banter and the natural, loving chaos of family life. The laughter in these moments is not at Andy's expense, but rather a reflection of the growing bond between him and his children.

This evolution in humor is also evident in Andy's relationship with Grace. In their early interactions, the humor is often tinged with bitterness or sarcasm, reflecting the unresolved tension between them. However, as Andy begins to make amends for his past mistakes, the humor becomes warmer and more affectionate. Their conversations become less about sniping at each other and more about finding common ground, and the humor shifts accordingly. This change in tone reflects the healing that takes place in their relationship, as they move from estrangement to reconciliation.

The way humor evolves in *Goodrich* is a testament to the film's nuanced approach to character development. Rather than using humor simply as a way to entertain, the film uses it as a tool to show how the characters are changing over time. Andy's growth as a father and as a person is mirrored in the way the humor shifts from broad, situational comedy to more intimate, character-driven moments of laughter. This shift not only makes the humor feel more organic, but it also deepens the emotional impact of the film by showing how Andy's relationships are evolving.

Audience Engagement Through Laughter

One of the key functions of humor in *Goodrich* is its ability to engage the audience and keep the film's tone light, even when dealing with heavier themes like addiction, family conflict, and redemption. The use of humor makes the film more accessible to a broader demographic, allowing it to appeal to viewers who might otherwise find the subject matter too intense or emotionally draining.

By incorporating humor into the story, *Goodrich* creates moments of **relatability** that resonate with the audience. Many of the comedic scenes are drawn from the everyday struggles of parenting, such as dealing with children's tantrums, navigating school drop-offs, or trying to cook dinner without setting the kitchen on fire. These moments are familiar to anyone who has experienced the challenges of raising children, and they help to ground the film in reality. The humor in these scenes allows the audience to see themselves in the characters, making the film feel more personal and engaging.

Moreover, the humor in *Goodrich* serves as a **release valve** for the emotional tension that builds throughout the film. As Andy confronts his past mistakes and tries to rebuild his relationship with Grace, the film touches on serious emotional themes that could easily overwhelm the audience. However, the use of humor ensures that these moments of tension are balanced with moments of levity, preventing the film from becoming too heavy or oppressive. The humor provides the audience with a sense of emotional relief, allowing them to process the more serious aspects of the story without feeling bogged down by the weight of the material.

The **accessibility** of the film's humor also broadens its appeal to different demographics. While the film deals with adult themes like addiction, divorce, and estrangement, the humor makes it enjoyable for a wider audience, including those who may not have experienced these specific challenges. The comedic elements help to soften the edges of the film's more difficult subject matter, making it easier for viewers to engage with the story. This balance between light and dark ensures that *Goodrich* remains entertaining while still addressing important emotional truths.

In addition to engaging the audience, the humor in *Goodrich* also contributes to the film's **emotional impact**. Laughter is often a gateway to deeper emotions, and the film uses this to great effect. By making the audience laugh, *Goodrich* creates a sense of connection with the characters, making their emotional struggles and triumphs feel more impactful. When Andy finally begins to repair his relationship with Grace, or when he starts to connect with his twins on a deeper level, the emotional weight of these moments is heightened by the laughter that has come before. The humor makes the characters feel more human, and this humanity makes their emotional journeys all the more moving.

In *Goodrich*, humor plays a crucial role in balancing the film's dramatic elements with lighter, more accessible moments. By skillfully blending comedy with emotionally driven scenes, the film avoids becoming overly heavy despite its exploration of themes like family conflict, addiction, and personal redemption. The humor in *Goodrich* reflects Andy's character growth, shifting from broad, situational comedy to more intimate, relational humor as he becomes more engaged with his children and begins to rebuild his relationships. This evolution in humor not only mirrors the emotional arc of the film but also deepens the audience's connection to the characters.

Moreover, the use of humor helps to engage the audience and make the...audience more emotionally invested in their journeys. The film's comedic elements prevent it from becoming too emotionally overwhelming, allowing viewers to experience both laughter and deeper emotional catharsis. By striking this balance, *Goodrich* appeals to a broad range of audiences, making its story of family, redemption, and personal growth both accessible and impactful. Ultimately, humor in *Goodrich* is not just a means of entertainment but a critical storytelling tool that enriches the film's emotional depth and resonance.

CONCLUSION

A Deep Dive into *Goodrich* – Family, Redemption, and Emotional Growth

Goodrich is more than a typical family drama—it is a poignant exploration of contemporary family dynamics, the complexity of parenting, and the universal struggle for redemption. Directed by Hallie Meyers-Shyer, the film's strength lies in its ability to skillfully balance humor with deeply emotional, often painful, themes. Through its compelling characters, especially Andy Goodrich (played by Michael Keaton), and its nuanced handling of complex issues like addiction, estrangement, and the difficulties of modern parenthood, *Goodrich* emerges as a thought-provoking narrative that resonates on multiple levels.

A Relatable and Timely Story of Modern Families

At the heart of *Goodrich* is the story of a man forced to confront the shortcomings of his past while attempting to reshape his future. The film's portrayal of family structures reflects the reality of many families today—blended, fractured, and imperfect. Andy's relationship with his children and his journey toward self-improvement mirror the challenges faced by many contemporary parents who find themselves trying to balance the demands of work, personal growth, and familial obligations.

The film's central themes are highly relevant to today's society. The notion of single parenthood, for example, is addressed with both humor and honesty, as Andy struggles to adapt to the responsibilities of raising his children on his own. His initial ineptitude and frustration are tempered by moments of connection and growth, underscoring the reality that parenting is often a process of trial and error. Andy's journey is one that many parents can relate to—learning to juggle work and personal responsibilities while striving to be a better, more engaged parent.

Additionally, *Goodrich* addresses the impact of addiction on families in a way that is both empathetic and authentic. The film doesn't sensationalize Andy's wife's struggle with addiction but presents it as a fact of life that families must cope with. Her absence from much of the film allows the focus to remain on Andy's personal transformation, but her influence is felt throughout, particularly in the emotional toll her addiction takes on the family unit. In this way, *Goodrich* tackles the complex interplay between addiction, recovery, and family dynamics, offering a compassionate portrayal of how these issues affect not just individuals, but the people who love and support them.

Character Development: Growth Through Humor and Heart

One of the defining features of *Goodrich* is its well-crafted character development, particularly with Andy. At the beginning of the film, Andy is depicted as a man who is disconnected from his children and overwhelmed by the prospect of caring for them on his own. His emotional distance from both his younger children and his adult daughter, Grace, is the primary source of tension in the film, and his journey toward redemption is marked by small, incremental steps rather than grand gestures.

What makes Andy's character arc so compelling is the realism with which it is portrayed. His growth as a father doesn't happen overnight—it's a slow, often awkward process, filled with moments of doubt, frustration, and humor. Early in the film, much of the comedy comes from Andy's clumsy attempts at parenting, as he struggles to manage basic tasks like getting his children to school on time or preparing meals without burning them. These moments of humor not only provide levity but also serve to highlight Andy's emotional growth. As the film progresses, the humor shifts, reflecting Andy's increasing competence and emotional connection with his children.

Grace's character arc is equally important to the film's emotional core. Her relationship with Andy is strained, primarily due to the resentment she harbors toward him for being absent during her childhood. However, Grace is not portrayed as one-dimensional—she is a strong, independent woman who is also vulnerable and hurt by her father's neglect. The film's portrayal of their relationship is nuanced and avoids the trap of easy reconciliation. Instead, it shows that healing takes time and requires effort on both sides. Grace's eventual willingness to forgive Andy is a testament to the film's belief in the possibility of redemption and the power of family bonds.

The Skillful Use of Humor to Balance Drama

A key strength of *Goodrich* is its ability to blend humor with the more serious, emotionally driven moments of the film. The film doesn't shy away from the difficult themes it explores, such as addiction, estrangement, and the challenges of modern parenting. However, it tempers these heavier moments with well-placed humor, preventing the film from becoming too heavy or melodramatic.

The humor in *Goodrich* is rooted in the characters and their situations, rather than relying on cheap gags or over-the-top antics. Much of the comedy arises from Andy's attempts to navigate the unfamiliar terrain of single parenthood. His mistakes and misunderstandings provide moments of levity, but they also serve to deepen the audience's connection to his character. We laugh at Andy's bumbling efforts because they are relatable and grounded in reality, and because we can see ourselves in his struggles.

As the film progresses, the humor evolves alongside the characters. Early on, the humor is broad and situational, reflecting Andy's discomfort and ineptitude. But as Andy grows more confident in his role as a father, the humor becomes more relational, arising from the interactions between him and his children. This shift mirrors Andy's emotional growth and helps to underscore the film's broader themes of connection, forgiveness, and family healing.

Cinematic Choices: Direction, Cinematography, and Music

Hallie Meyers-Shyer's direction is marked by its focus on character-driven storytelling and its refusal to rely on melodrama or emotional manipulation. Instead, the film's emotional beats are allowed to unfold naturally, with the characters' interactions and dialogue taking center stage. Meyers-Shyer's approach is subtle, allowing the audience to connect with the characters in an organic way, rather than forcing them into moments of high drama.

The cinematography by Jamie D. Ramsay complements the film's emotional tone, using soft, natural lighting to create a warm, inviting atmosphere. The contrast between the cool, sterile lighting of Andy's art gallery and the warmer tones used in the family home visually represents the emotional shift that takes place over the course of the film. As Andy becomes more involved in his children's lives, the film's visual palette becomes warmer and more intimate, reflecting the growing connection between him and his family.

Christopher Willis's musical score is another highlight of the film, enhancing the emotional resonance of key moments without overwhelming the narrative. The score shifts between light, playful melodies during the film's more comedic scenes and more somber, reflective tones during moments of emotional tension. This balance mirrors the film's overall tone, blending humor and heart in a way that feels both authentic and engaging.

Cultural and Social Relevance

In addition to its personal, character-driven story, *Goodrich* also has broader cultural and social relevance. The film's exploration of addiction, single parenthood, and the evolving roles of fathers in modern families speaks to contemporary societal issues. By portraying Andy as a man who is learning to balance his professional life with the demands of fatherhood, the film reflects the reality of many parents today who are trying to juggle multiple responsibilities while striving to be present in their children's lives.

The film's handling of addiction is particularly timely, given the ongoing discussions around mental health and substance abuse in today's society. By showing how addiction impacts not just the individual but also their family, *Goodrich* offers a compassionate and realistic portrayal of a difficult issue. The film's emphasis on seeking help and working toward recovery also sends a positive message about the importance of addressing addiction in a supportive and understanding way.

Lasting Impact and Potential for Recognition

The emotional resonance of *Goodrich* is likely to have a lasting impact on viewers, particularly those who have experienced similar struggles in their own families. The film's message of redemption, forgiveness, and the possibility of second chances is a powerful one, and it is delivered in a way that feels both genuine and hopeful.

While *Goodrich* may not have the blockbuster appeal of larger, more commercial films, its strength lies in its emotional honesty and its ability to connect with audiences on a personal level. Michael Keaton's performance as Andy has been widely praised for its depth and nuance, and there is potential for the film to receive recognition in awards circuits, particularly in categories like acting, writing, and direction.

In conclusion, *Goodrich* is a deeply moving film that explores the complexities of family, personal growth, and redemption with humor and heart. Through its well-drawn characters, skillful use of humor, and nuanced handling of difficult themes, the film offers a compelling narrative that resonates with contemporary audiences. Andy Goodrich's journey toward becoming a better father and a more emotionally present individual is a testament to the film's central message—that it is never too late to change, to seek forgiveness, and to rebuild relationships. With its warm, naturalistic cinematography, thoughtful direction, and emotionally evocative score, *Goodrich* is a film that will leave a lasting impression on viewers, offering both laughter and tears in equal measure.

www.ingramcontent.com/pod-product-compliance
Lightning Source LLC
Chambersburg PA
CBHW070351230526
45471CB00006B/2517